*G*len Canyon National Recreation Area and Lake Powell were unknown to many people, even residents of nearby states, a few years ago. All of that has changed. Now, over 3.1 million people journey to Glen Canyon-Lake Powell each year. They are attracted by the irresistible charm of warm summer days, cool lake water, and spectacular vistas — all ideal for many forms of recreation and outdoor enjoyment.

This land is *"...a curious ensemble of wonderful features—carved walls, royal arches, glens, alcove gulches, mounds and monuments... We decide to call it Glen Canyon."*

John Wesley Powell, 1869.

Glen Canyon National Recreation Area, *located in south central Utah and north central Arizona, was established in 1972. Lake Powell stretches 186 miles behind the dam.*

Front Cover: Gunsight Butte at sunset, photo by Gary Ladd. Inside Front Cover: Rainbow Bridge and reflection, photo by Gary Ladd. Page 1: Iceberg Canyon, photo by Dick Dietrich. Pages 2/3: Lake Powell sunrise from Lake Shore Drive, photo by Gary Ladd. Pages 4/5: Castle Rock from near Wahweap Marina, photo by Gary Ladd.

Edited by Cheri C. Madison.
Book design by K. C. DenDooven.

Second Printing, 1994
in pictures GLEN CANYON - LAKE POWELL The Continuing Story
© 1992 KC PUBLICATIONS, INC.

LC 92-70429. ISBN 0-88714-066-1.

in pictures

Glen Canyon -Lake Powell

The Continuing Story®

by Denny Davies

Denny Davies, a native of New Mexico, has spent 28 years with the National Park Service. His 3 years at Glen Canyon gave him a deep yearning to share the secrets of this magnificent land with any who would pause to look, feel, listen, or just revel in being alive.

*N*ational park areas are special landscapes set aside by acts of Congress to protect and preserve features of national significance that are generally categorized as scenic, scientific, historical, and recreational.

As Americans, we are joint caretakers of these unique places, and we gladly share them with visitors from around the world.

Lake Powell is the star attraction of Glen Canyon National Recreation Area. The lake is 186 miles long; features 96 major side canyons; and has 1,960 miles of shoreline — longer than the west coast of the continental United States! Yet, in spite of its huge size, the lake comprises only 13 percent of the park's 1.25 million acres. Hidden within side canyons or clustered behind towering cliffs are some of the most rugged, beautiful and remote attractions of the plateau country of northern Arizona and southern Utah. Glen Canyon is a treasure-trove of fascinating sights, sounds, and sensations — all just waiting for your discovery.

GARY LADD

Cascading rivulets and reflective pools are unexpected surprises in side canyons of this desert region.

The Land...The Canyon...The Lake

Over 10 million years ago, the Glen Canyon landscape was much different than it is today. After millennia of relative stability, dramatic events began changing the face of western America. Forces deep within the earth caused the land to rise dramatically. As the land rose, the ancestral Colorado River was able to cut into the land, retaining its basic course to the Gulf of Mexico. Over time, stream channels widened and thousands of *cubic miles* of earth were worn away by water and the relentless forces of nature. What resulted is the maze of canyons, plateaus, and spires that make this country the visitor mecca it is today.

After millions of years of wild flows, the Colorado was changed forever in 1956 when construction began on the Glen Canyon Dam. The dam was completed in 1963 and Lake Powell began filling. Seventeen years later, in 1980 after several extremely wet years, the lake filled to capacity. The 186-mile-long Lake Powell is now the destination resort for millions of visitors. People from all around the world flock to Lake Powell to revel in the stark contrast of blue water, red sandstone cliffs, and the beautiful, cloud-studded sky of this desert oasis.

◄ **P**rior to formation of Lake Powell, the Colorado River gorge was a major obstacle to travel and settlement of this region. In November 1879, 250 Mormon pioneers arrived at this spot they later called "Hole-in-the-Rock." They were searching for a short cut to the fertile valleys of southeastern Utah. Trapped by heavy winter snows, the party faced the monumental task of building a "road" down a 45-degree slope to the river over a thousand feet below. For the next 60 days, they cribbed, blasted, and dug a wagon path. In late January 1880, they successfully moved 38 wagons, livestock, and all their belongings to the riverbank less than a mile away. This epic journey will forever remain a testament to a determined people.

The elevation of Glen Canyon ▶ National Recreation Area varies from 3,000 feet above sea level to over 7,800 feet on the Kaiparowits Plateau. From the north flank of Navajo Mountain, the hiker gets a fantastic view of Lake Powell, its rugged terrain, and the Kaiparowits Plateau only a few miles to the northwest. Spectacular Rainbow Bridge is very close to this spot.

GARY LADD

▲ **The Glen Canyon area is part of the Great Basin desert. But, climatically speaking, what is a desert?** *One simple definition: A desert is any place that receives less than 12 inches of precipitation per year. About half of Glen Canyon's precipitation falls as snow. The remaining portion falls as rain, often in summer as brief, and sometimes violent thunderstorms. Such was the case when this picture was taken in Coyote Gulch, one of the tributaries of the Escalante River. It's here that hikers find some of the spectacular natural bridges and arches located in the recreation area.*

One often thinks of deserts ▶ *as being barren and lifeless. Fortunately, that is not the case. Through millions of years of change, plants and animals have adapted to the harsh environment of the desert. Here, seeds of the chinch weed found a favorable location and were watered by the runoff of a fall storm. Under the right conditions, seeds are produced and survival of the species is ensured.*

GARY LADD

Water: The Great Carver

Of all the forces ▶ of nature, water erosion is the most conspicuous in this arid land. As water runs downhill, it abrades, scours, and tumbles other material in a relentless assault on the landscape. Granular sandstone, so common around Lake Powell, is no match for the cutting action of water—the great carver. Small, intermittent streams like this one near Page, Arizona, can become raging torrents during flash floods caused by summer downpours. Visitors are urged to avoid all stream courses when rains threaten.

San Juan —
A River Joins a Lake

◀ **Upstream from Lake Powell, the**
Colorado and San Juan rivers provide thrilling
opportunities for white-water recreation. This
kayaker in the San Juan is dwarfed by the
immensity of the canyons.

From the air, one can see the lower end of the ▶
San Juan near its confluence with the main channel
of Lake Powell. This photo, taken on a November late
afternoon, begins to convey the many moods of the
lake. The view is toward the southeast
in the direction of Monument Valley

▼ **An aerial view shows why this**
section of river is called "Goosenecks of the
San Juan." It is just upstream from the
recreation area and is part of the Utah state
park system. Goosenecks State Park can be
reached on Utah Highway 316 near
Mexican Hat, Utah.

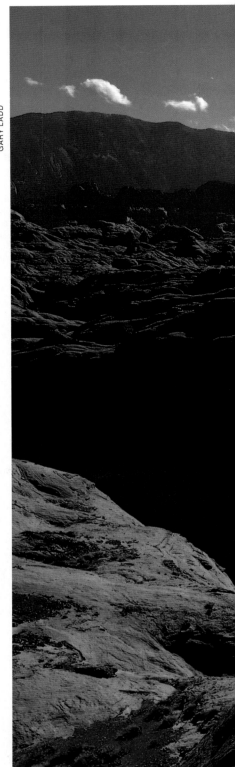

The Lake

◀ **Visitors to Lake Powell are**
wise to rise early (this is sunrise
from the road to Wahweap) or
be out at dusk. Long shadows and
brilliant contrasts reward
alert observers at this
magical oasis.

▲ **Lake Powell is one of the star attractions of the National Park System. Nowhere else in the world** *can the boater be confronted with a more fantastic array of scenery than is found at Glen Canyon. Lake Powell is the second largest man-made body of water in the United States. It features 96 major side canyons just waiting for discovery. The shoreline stretches for almost 2,000 miles and provides wonderful places to camp, fish, water-ski, and swim — or just enjoy the contrast of azure water, red cliffs, and spectacular skies. In this scene, the 50-foot houseboat is dwarfed by the immensity of its surroundings. Navajo Mountain rises to almost 10,400 feet above sea level. Because of its size, Navajo Mountain can be seen from many locations and serves as a friendly landmark to boaters traversing the lake.*

Marinas — Where the Adventure Begins

Marinas like Halls ▶
Crossing are where boating adventures begin. Operated by a private concessioner, the lake's five marinas provide fuel, groceries, fishing supplies, and even rental of houseboats or smaller runabouts.

◀ **Dangling Rope Marina is the only** marina located mid-lake between Wahweap and Bullfrog. Each year, this fueling station services tens of thousands of boaters. Dangling Rope gets its name from an old miner's rope that was found in a nearby canyon.

GARY LADD

GARY LADD

▲ **The ferryboat "John Atlantic Burr"** provides transportation daily throughout the year between Bullfrog and Halls Crossing. The 25 minute trip covers 7 miles and saves a drive of 160 miles through Hite, Utah. The ferry operates only during daylight hours. Visitors are urged to check the schedule before beginning a trip.

▲ **W**ahweap Marina, 7 miles
north of Page, is the oldest and
busiest marina on Lake Powell. It is
home for almost a thousand privately
owned boats plus the largest rental
fleet of houseboats and smaller
runabouts on the lake. Wahweap is
a full-service, year-round resort.

Prior to 1970, this area was ▷
open country with only an occasional
hardy visitor. With the filling of Lake
Powell, however, Bullfrog Marina
sprung to life and is now the second
largest development on the lake. The
Henry Mountains form a spectacular
backdrop for Bullfrog. They remind us
that in the recent geologic past, this
area was unstable and changed
dramatically. About 48 million years
ago, molten rock welled up from deep
inside the earth, creating both the
Henry and Navajo mountains.

SCOTT T. SMITH

▲ **Jacob Hamblin Arch is one** of three major arches in Coyote Gulch. Because of spectacular arches, pristine beauty, and ancient Indian ruins, the Escalante River region was proposed as a national park as early as 1937. Although that proposal never bore fruit, much of the land was incorporated into the recreation area in 1972 when Glen Canyon was created by an act of Congress.

Just downstream from the ▶ Hamblin arch is the beautiful Stevens Arch, also located in the Escalante drainage. Hikers' access to the Escalante can be gained by vehicle over Hole-in-the-Rock Road or by hiking upstream from the edge of Lake Powell.

SCOTT T. SMITH

18

Escalante — Land of Arches

SCOTT T. SMITH

Natural bridges like Coyote
Bridge are carved by running water. The
water in canyons like this supports a
community of plants and animals that
would be impossible without the life-
giving effect of this precious desert
commodity. Highlighted by the radiant
sun, cottonwood trees are bathed
in shimmering beauty.

La Gorce Arch in Davis Gulch (also in ▷
the Escalante) is a favorite destination for
boaters. Some of the canyons are quite narrow
and require skillful operation and alertness for
obstacles and other boats. Arches like La Gorce
are formed as the result of complex processes
and differential weathering of narrow
fins of rock.

GARY LADD

 **Descriptive phrases seem to fail when it** comes to describing Rainbow Bridge — its beauty and significance. Rainbow Bridge is one of the most graceful, beautiful, and awe-inspiring features of the natural world. At 290 feet high with a span of 275 feet, it is so large that the U.S. Capitol could fit beneath it! Its appearance changes with the seasons, with the time of day; it is ever-changing, yet somehow timeless. When first recorded by explorers in 1909, the bridge was one of the most isolated natural treasures in the United States. However, with the filling of Lake Powell, it is now the destination stop for a quarter million boaters annually. Many people now favor tighter controls and restricted access to help preserve this natural wonder.

Navajo trader John Weatherill was with the Cummings-Douglass parties in 1909. Word of Rainbow Bridge spread rapidly after this journey.

Rainbow Bridge

▲ *A **close-up view of the top of Rainbow Bridge reveals its massiveness — it's 42 feet thick** (top to bottom) and 33 feet wide (side to side). Now try to find the bridge in the photo below.*

◀ ***T**he north slope of Navajo Mountain is a maze of incised canyons, intersecting ridges, and numerous alcoves. In spite of its size and distinctive appearance, Rainbow Bridge is difficult to spot from far away. Have you located it yet? (Look closely at the bottom left portion of the picture.) This view helps give scale to the size and expansive nature of Glen Canyon National Recreation Area.*

GARY LADD

Glen Canyon Dam

◀ **In its tumultuous history, the Colorado River**
has ranged from a placid stream supporting over
11,000 years of human history to a raging torrent
wreaking havoc on the land and anything in its path.
In 1956 to control its flows and provide hydroelectric
power for an expanding population, Congress
authorized construction of Glen Canyon Dam. For
seven years, thousands of workers labored around
the clock to build the fourth-highest dam in the
United States. When the by-pass tunnels were
closed in 1963, Lake Powell began to form. Because
of both up-river and down-river water requirements,
skeptics doubted that the lake would ever fill.
However, fill it did for the first time in 1980. Because
of a design flaw in the spillways and several
extraordinarily wet years, emergency measures were
needed in 1983 and 1984 to keep the lake from
overflowing the dam. In this picture from June 1983,
four jet valves, both spillways, and all eight
generators were working at maximum allowable
capacity. The measures worked and water
never overflowed the dam.

Prior to the construction of the ▲
Glen Canyon Dam, this area was one of
the most remote places in the United
States. There were no paved roads, and
scattered groups of Navajo Indians were
the only inhabitants. All that changed in
1956 with the construction of the dam.
One of the engineers' first obstacles was
to construct a bridge across Glen Canyon,
which is over 700 feet deep at this
location and one-third mile wide. This
bridge now carries traffic on U.S. 89
between Arizona and Utah. The National
Park Service operates a visitor center at
the west end of the dam (building with
rotunda) where visitors can get
information on the NRA.

Overleaf: Reds, purples, ▶
and blues combine to make Glen
Canyon a spectacular showcase!
Photo by Jeff Gnass.

23

Life Along the Edge

Glen Canyon is located on the Colorado Plateau, a vast tableland covering roughly 150,000 square miles of northern Arizona, northwestern New Mexico, western Colorado, and most of southern and eastern Utah. The plateau varies in elevation from a low of 1,200 feet along the Colorado River in the Grand Canyon to over 12,000 feet in the San Juan Mountains of southwestern Colorado. The climate is arid and humidity is low (generally less than 40 percent). Because of its mean elevation and position in the northern latitudes, the Glen Canyon area is classified as a "cold" desert with all areas receiving snow during the winter months. All of these factors — arid climate, low humidity, and high desert — dictate a unique combination of life forms that has evolved over millions of years. Temperatures in the park vary from sub-freezing during the winter months to about 100° F in July and August. Although the lake water cools dramatically in the winter, surface temperatures rise to a comfortable 82° F in the summer — perfect for all water sports.

The presence of cattails in Coyote Gulch indicates a constant supply of moisture in this canyon. Such streams are relatively rare in Utah's canyon country, but are extremely valuable because of the life forms they support. Drainages like this are called riparian zones and are excellent locations for viewing wildlife.

Desert plants have many adaptations which ensure survival in this harsh, high-desert environment. Evening primrose, shown here in late May, bloom after the heat of the day subsides, reducing water loss through evaporation. Tower Butte, just east of Page, Arizona, is prominent in the background.

TOM TILL

Birds at Glen Canyon

Once Lake Powell was created, the variety of birds that inhabit these canyons (or which stop during their migration) increased markedly. Over the last few years, visitors and staff have recorded nearly 200 different species at various locations throughout the park.

Golden eagles are year-round ▶ residents of the canyon country. They are an important link in nature's "web of life." Eagles prey principally on rodents and other small wildlife. Note the bone from a fawn's leg.

JOHN P. GEORGE

KRIS ILLENBERGER

◀ **T**he Muscovy duck was originally found from Mexico to South America. As with other waterfowl, however, the Muscovy has been domesticated and its range extended. This one was seen at Wahweap Marina.

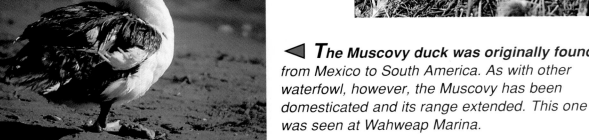

The great ▶ horned owl, depicted here in a defensive posture, is the largest owl in North America with ear tufts. These feathery tufts give it the name "horned" owl.

JOHN P. GEORGE

Like its near-relative the ▷
mockingbird, this sage thrasher is
a great mimicker of other birds.
Its songs are loud and are
repeated two or three times.
The thrasher is a common summer
bird on the Colorado Plateau. Its
long, slender beak is ideal for
capturing insects.

JOHN P. GEORGE

◁ **K**illdeer are shorebirds that have
adapted to open prairie and desert. With
their camouflaged colors, they blend
easily into their surroundings. This one
is in a display posture, used in courtship or
when threatened. Killdeer are famous
for their "broken wing" act, feigning injury
with loud cries while moving away from
their ground nest.

JOHN P. GEORGE

JOHN P. GEORGE

Burrowing owls are small owls with long legs ▷
and no ear tufts. The lack of bold spots and "bars" on
the breast distinguish these as immature birds.
When full-grown, an adult is only 9 to 10 inches
long! Burrowing owls migrate from the Glen Canyon
region each fall and return each spring to breed. They
nest in abandoned burrows and can commonly
be seen standing by their burrow during
daylight hours.

Desert Wildlife

Different from the deserts of southern California and southern Arizona, the desert region of Glen Canyon is considered a "cold" desert. High elevations (averaging over 5,000 feet above sea level) and the freezing temperatures of winter create harsh conditions that dictate a hardy variety of desert wildlife.

JOHN P. GEORGE

▲ **Commonly called a "horned toad," this** creature is actually a short-horned lizard. Its spines or horns are excellent defensive protection for these slow-moving desert dwellers. Because of their slow pace, these lizards have been easy prey for collectors and are now protected under the laws of most western states.

JOHN P. GEORGE

▲ *The canyon tree* frog is one of only two frogs native to the Glen Canyon region. It lives in moist canyons or plunge pools where it is usually nocturnal, but becomes active in daylight after summer rains.

Folklore has given ▷ tarantulas a bad rap. Though they are mildly poisonous, their mouth parts are small and they pose little threat to humans. Their primary prey are insects.

GARY LADD

The Web of Life

In nature there are no  "good guys" or "bad guys." All creatures occupy a unique spot in the web of life. In this web are herbivores — animals that eat plants, and carnivores that prey on other animals. None is more deserving than the others; each is dependent on others in a complex association. Coyotes are one of the most adaptable and successful carnivores in the West. Without them and other predators, rodents would soon overrun the country.

JOHN P. GEORGE

JOHN P. GEORGE

GARY LADD

▲ **Probably the most maligned and misunderstood creature in the animal world is the snake. As far** ▲ back as Biblical times, this creature had an unfortunate and undeserved reputation. Glen Canyon is home to 13 species of snakes including the gopher snake on the left and the western rattlesnake on the right. Rattlesnakes are the only poisonous snakes in the park. All snakes are extremely beneficial and prey on insects, small mammals, eggs, and birds. They are generally shy and avoid confrontation with non-prey animals (including you and me) whenever possible.

◄ *The collared lizard is one of the most common reptiles of the canyon country. This species grows to a length of 14 inches and can be easily recognized by the black collars encircling the neck.*

KRIS ILLENBERGER

All scorpions are ►
poisonous, but with few exceptions, the one found here is not deadly to humans. Scorpions use their tail-stinger to immobilize their prey — usually insects. They are found under rocks, rotting wood, or desert litter and are generally very shy. However, their sting can be quite painful, so beware!

GARY LADD

▲ **It's a major thrill to see a** desert bighorn on the canyon slopes. Only mature rams develop full-curl horns. These sheep are known for their rock-climbing ability. They range widely over large areas and are frequently depicted in prehistoric Indian rock art.

Porcupines have highly ▷ specialized "hair" which takes the form of spines and quills. The quills provide excellent defense against most predators, an important fact for this slow-moving member of the rodent family. Porcupines live almost entirely by eating tender twigs or the bark of trees and shrubs. They rarely "girdle" (eat all the way around) the vegetation they feed on, which ensures survival of both them and their host plants.

GARY LADD

33

PETER KRESAN

Flowers Too are Desert Life

Readers not familiar with Glen Canyon will be surprised at the variety of the park's plant life. Because of its topography and an elevation range of almost 5,000 feet, the park is a true outdoor museum of botanical diversity.

◀ *When one thinks of deserts, cacti are often the first plants to come to mind. This hedgehog cactus is one of many species found in Glen Canyon. Hedgehog form mounds, sometimes with as many as 50 stems in a single group. When in full bloom (May through July), these large mounds form a mass of bright flowers. Once freed of its spines, the yellow-green fruit is succulent and edible.*

GARY LADD

◀ *The large, showy dock is found along arroyos (dry washes) and road shoulders. It is a perennial that reaches a height of 24 to 30 inches and blossoms in March and April. Navajo Indians use the tannin extracted from roots as natural dye in their beautiful, handmade wool rugs.*

34

▲ **T**he pretty blossoms of the spiderwort make this otherwise scraggly looking plant a desert delight. Flower colors range from pink to blue.

▲ **T**he Kanab prairie clover graces parts of the canyon country. It has a delicate flower, which can be seen beginning in April.

Different from many spring ▷ bloomers, the scarlet cardinal flower blossoms in September and October. These flowers are often found in moist alcoves called "hanging gardens."

◀ **T**he scorpionweed is a prominent, showy plant of the Southwest. It gets its name from the curled flower-head which resembles the flexed tail of a scorpion.

Glen Canyon National Recreation Area

In 1972 with Lake Powell over half-full and rising, the recreation area was formally established as a unit of the national park system on October 27 of that year. Originally, planners forecast that annual visitation would rise to half a million by the year 2000. They were much too conservative — that level was reached in just 7 years! Today, over 3.1 million visitors seek out Glen Canyon and Lake Powell each year. The park encompasses 1.25 million acres and includes all of Lake Powell, 96 major side canyons, countless coves and bays, and almost 2,000 miles of shoreline. With its magical backdrop of colorful canyons, blue sky, and long summers, Lake Powell takes center stage as the premiere attraction of the recreation area.

Lake Powell is now a destination resort for people from all over the world. The park is within one day's drive from such urban centers as Albuquerque, Phoenix, Los Angeles, San Diego, Las Vegas, Salt Lake City, and Denver. Between 1980 and 1988, visitation to the area grew by over 8 percent a year, from 1.65 million to 3.25 million! These visitors have all discovered the scenic and recreation riches of this land first explored by the lake's namesake, John Wesley Powell, in 1869.

Because of the lake's charm and attributes, it's easy to see why water sports are the favorite form of recreation at Glen Canyon NRA. Visitors can choose boating, skiing, scuba diving, fishing, camping, or hiking — or all of these on the same trip! No wonder Glen Canyon-Lake Powell has become the major visitor mecca that it is today.

◀ **Lake Powell's** beautiful spring and fall seasons make its canyon country an ideal (and spectacular!) spot for mild-season hiking and backpacking. Page-based photographer Gary Ladd frequently joins a group of friends and outdoor enthusiasts for an annual Thanksgiving hike. Such was the case when Gary captured this slickrock scene in Balanced Rock Canyon, just uplake from Dangling Rope Marina.

PETER KRESAN

▲ **Water-skiing is one of the most popular water sports enjoyed on Lake** Powell. Skiers can attain speeds of 45-70 mph as they make their turns!

Boaters have ▶ a fantastic array of choices for their evening campsites. This party chose a secluded spot in the San Juan arm near some showy, trumpet-flowered Datura (also called thornapples).

DICK DIETRICH

◀ **One does not** have to get very far from the lake to find peace, solitude, and remarkable natural treasures. This March hiker pauses at a pool left over after a spring storm in a canyon near Navajo Mountain. Occasionally, springs surface on the sandstone walls as they have here. The resultant staining is striking and beautiful. Such discoveries await anyone who invests a little time and effort.

GARY LADD

A Land of Varied Adventure

▲ **L**ake Powell draws large numbers of family groups for summer vacations. For children of all ages, building sand castles is a fun form of artistic expression.

▲ **W**ith the advantage of compressed ir, these scuba divers were able to explore ace Canyon for extended periods. Clear ater and warm temperatures made their ugust trip a delightful underwater dventure.

Photography is another popular ▶ recreational activity. With its colorful assets and rugged terrain, the Glen Canyon-Lake Powell area is a photographer's dreamland. Each year, photography workshops like this one gather students eager to stretch the limits of their artistic excellence.

▲ **P**arasailing is a
new form of water sport.
This "flier" is being towed
by the boat, tethered
at the end of a long rope.
Parasailers say it is an
exhilarating, never-to-
be-forgotten experience!

Weather on Lake ▷
Powell in October is
fabulous! Warm days and
cool nights (and fewer
visitors) make early fall an
ideal time to visit. This
sailboat ties up for the night
near Gregory Butte and
West Canyon.

▲ **Scenic flights are a wonderful way to get a park overview. Flying helps compress the** immensity of the recreation area while providing breathtaking perspectives that would be impossible from the ground or water level. These cliffs rise 700 to 1,200 feet above Lake Powell. Charter flights are available year-round at the Page, Arizona, airport.

GARY LADD

GARY LADD

GARY LADD

▲ **D**ifferential erosion, fracturing, and natural cementation create unique "boxwork" in a sandstone layer on the flanks of Navajo Mountain. Hikers should always use care to protect the park's delicate features.

▲ **T**he Glen Canyon area was home for the prehistoric people we now call the "Anasazi," the Ancient Ones. Scattered throughout the region are ruins left by these people who suddenly abandoned their homes around A.D. 1200. All ruins are fragile and need our protection. Defiance House ruins near Bullfrog have been restored.

Dinosaurs once ruled the earth and ▶ were common here on what is now called the Colorado Plateau. Approximately 150 million years ago, a group of Brontosaurus-like dinosaurs walked across a mud flat leaving these footprints. The prints were later fossilized and are now preserved in stone.

▲ **No matter the season or the weather, Glen Canyon and Lake Powell hold a powerful attraction for** *all who come to this remarkable area. Heavy November rains create a somber mood as this houseboat plies the water near Dangling Rope. For their own safety, boaters should check weather conditions, have a good map, know the boating regulations, and be prepared to seek protective shelter when conditions dictate.*

Glen Canyon Natural History Association

Established in 1988, the Glen Canyon NHA is a nonprofit corporation that provides support and funding for various educational, interpretive, and research activities within the park. These include a "Coffee with the Ranger" program at Wahweap and Bullfrog campgrounds, a Junior Ranger program complete with membership buttons, daily guided tours through Glen Canyon Dam (on a seasonal basis), and the permanent staffing at visitor centers in two states—Arizona and Utah. They also maintain a cooperative agreement with the BLM for the sale of publications in the Paria Wilderness Area and Kanab, Utah.

To assist the many international visitors, the Association had the National Recreation Area's brochures translated into French and German and distributed throughout the park.

SUGGESTED READINGS

Barnes, F. A. *Utah Canyon Country.* Salt Lake City, Utah: Utah Geographic Series, Inc., 1986.

Everhart, Ronald E. *Glen Canyon-Lake Powell: The Story Behind the Scenery.* Las Vegas, Nevada: KC Publications, Inc., 1983.

Mac Mahon, James A. *Deserts. The Audubon Society Nature Guides.* New York, New York: Alfred A. Knopf, 1990 (Fifth Printing).

Murphy, Dan. *John Wesley Powell, Voyage of Discovery: The Story Behind the Scenery.* Las Vegas, Nevada: KC Publications, Inc., 1991.

Netoff, Dennis et al. *The Lake Powell Boater's Guide.* Page, Arizona: Glen Canyon Natural History Association, 1989.

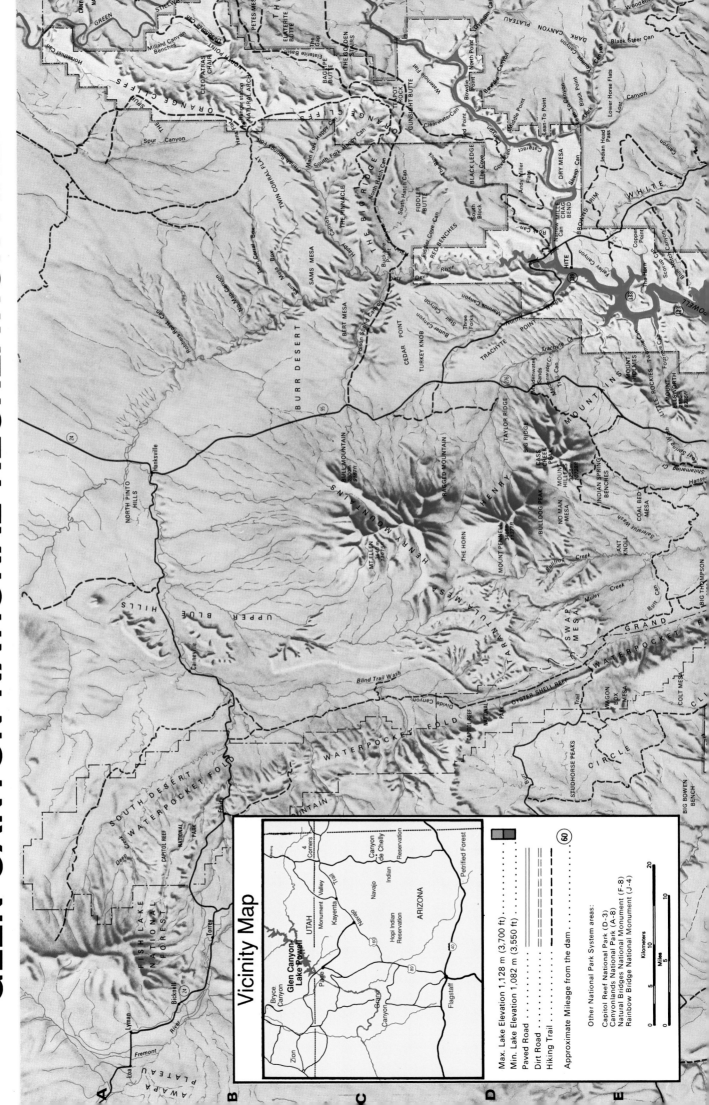

GLEN CANYON NATIONAL RECREATION AREA

Vicinity Map

Max. Lake Elevation 1,128 m (3,700 ft) ....
Min. Lake Elevation 1,082 m (3,550 ft) ....
Paved Road ....
Dirt Road ....
Hiking Trail ....

Approximate Mileage from the dam. ⑥⓪

Other National Park System areas:

Capitol Reef National Park (D-3)
Canyonlands National Park (A-8)
Natural Bridges National Monument (F-8)
Rainbow Bridge National Monument (J-4)

Kilometers
Miles

GARY LADD

It's our hope that your journey through this *Continuing Story* has been an adventure, an exploration of one of our nation's premiere national parks. Glen Canyon National Recreation Area features a fantastic array of diverse resources. For the outdoor enthusiast, the park offers superb water-based recreation. For the hiker, the canyons and mesas offer unparalleled challenges and opportunities. The park is also a mecca for history buffs curious about man's struggle to survive during the last 11,000 years. And finally, the park is an outdoor museum and study area for everyone interested in the fragile balance of nature in a desert environment.

Whatever your interest, we hope you will agree that you find it all the more rewarding because of the magnificent setting of Glen Canyon-Lake Powell. This area is uniquely blessed with some of the most colorful and beautiful terrain in North America. It's waiting for *your* discovery!

Even in winter, the charm of Glen Canyon captures our imagination and kindles our spirits.

47

GARY LADD

▲ **There is no end to the opportunities for exploration and discovery in Glen Canyon-**
Lake Powell. These hikers have located a deep alcove in a side canyon near Navajo
Mountain. Moments like these are fleeting and should be savored for a long time.

Inside back cover: Slot ▶
canyons carved by running water are
some of earth's most special places.
Photo by John P. George.

Back cover: Nine-mile Bar ▶
overlook shows the Colorado River
below the dam. Photo by Gary Ladd.

Books in this in pictures ... The Continuing Story series are: Arches & Canyonlands,
Bryce Canyon, Death Valley, Everglades, Glacier, Glen Canyon-Lake Powell, Grand Canyon,
Hawai'i Volcanoes, Mount Rainier, Mount St. Helens, Olympic, Petrified Forest,
Sequoia & Kings Canyon, Yellowstone, Yosemite, Zion.

Translation Packages are also available. Each title can be ordered with a booklet
in German, or French, or Japanese bound into the center of the English book.
Selected titles in this series as well as other KC Publications' books are available
in up to five additional languages.

The original national park series: The Story Behind the Scenery, covers over 75 parks
and related areas. A series on Indian culture is also available. To receive our catalog
listing over 90 titles:
Call (800-626-9673), fax (702-433-4320), or write to the address below.

Published by KC Publications, 3245 E. Patrick Ln., Suite A, Las Vegas, NV 89120.

Created, Designed and Published in the U.S.A.
Printed by Dong-A Printing and Publishing, Seoul, Korea
Color Separations by Kedia/Kwangyangsa Co., Ltd.